WALLSEND
THEN & NOW

IN COLOUR

ROB KIRKUP

The
History
Press

First published in 2014

The History Press
The Mill, Brimscombe Port
Stroud, Gloucestershire, GL5 2QG
www.thehistorypress.co.uk

British Library Cataloguing in Publication Data.
A catalogue record for this book is available from the British Library.

ISBN 978 0 7524 6561 6

Typesetting and origination by The History Press
Printed in India.

CONTENTS

ACKNOWLEDGEMENTS

I would like to thank my friends and family for all their support and words of encouragement while compiling *Wallsend Then & Now*. A special mention goes to my good friend Andrew Markwell, a fellow Wallsender, who accompanied me across the town taking the photos that you will see throughout these pages; all present-day images were taken by the author with an Olympus PEN E-PL1 camera.

A huge debt of gratitude goes to the kind people who supplied the archive images, and they are credited throughout.

INTRODUCTION

The very name of Wallsend highlights the beginning of the town, located in North Tyneside, as the Roman fort of Segedunum (meaning strong fort) was built here in AD 126 at the eastern end of Hadrian's Wall.

The first ever 'Wallsenders' settled outside the fort, and the community and settlement grew even after the Romans left in the fifth century. The ninth century brought the threat of Viking raids on the eastern coast, and with the settlement dangerously close to the River Tyne it was abandoned and a new settlement was formed on the site of the current Wallsend Green. Farms were built around the Green, with many of the buildings constructed from stone from the long-abandoned fort, and for centuries this would be the centre of the village, with the surrounding area used for farming. In around 1155 reclaimed stone from the fort was also used to construct Wallsend's first church; Holy Cross church was built atop a hill overlooking the Burn Closes to serve Wallsend village as well as the village of Willington.

In the 1780s, coal mining had come to Wallsend, which was still a village based around the Green, and had seven farms. Wallsend's coal soon became famous worldwide for its high quality, and this brought wealthy merchants from Newcastle-upon-Tyne, only 4 miles away, to Wallsend. Soon the farms were being bought up and demolished to make way for large country houses.

Wallsend was known as an industrial town, and this reputation was only strengthened towards the end of the 1800s when shipbuilding came to Wallsend. C.S. Swan & Hunter was formed in 1880 and would gain international recognition for building over 1,600 ships, including the RMS *Mauretania*, which held the Blue Riband for the fastest crossing of the Atlantic for twenty-two years, and the HMS *Ark Royal* in the 1980s, which would become the flagship of the Royal Navy.

In 1901 Wallsend was granted borough status, and in 1908 the Town Hall was opened. The year 1910 saw Willington Quay, Willington, Howdon, Battle Hill, part of Longbenton, and the Rising Sun Colliery, which had opened two years earlier, included within the expanded Wallsend Borough. In 1974 Wallsend Borough became part of North Tyneside Council, and the Town Hall would become the council's headquarters.

The 1900s saw Wallsend develop and grow, and this continued into the new millennium, despite the loss of both the shipbuilding and coal industries upon which it had thrived.

In 2000 the site that started it all – the newly excavated Roman fort of Segedunum – was opened to the public as the Segedunum Roman Fort, Baths & Museum, attracting visitors from all over the world to see the most completely excavated fort in Britain.

Wallsend benefits from a rich heritage, and there are over 42,000 people who are proud to call Wallsend home – and that includes me.

Rob Kirkup, 2014

ALLEN MEMORIAL METHODIST CHURCH

THE RED BRICK and sandstone-built Allen Memorial Methodist church was founded in 1903 and opened the following year, and is named for late local man John Allen. Allen was born in South Shields in 1791 and trained as a chemist before founding the Heworth Shore alkali works in 1828. He opened an alkali factory in Wallsend in 1847 and it was largely through his efforts that the Methodist New Connexion movement was

kick-started in the town; he donated a site for a Zion chapel on the north-east corner of Station Road and the High Street, together with £300 towards the construction, with the foundation stone being laid in 1857. He was an active supporter at the chapel until his death in 1860. His impact was so great that when the chapel was sold in 1903 and the current Methodist church opened, it was named for him. (Archive photograph provided by North Shields Library)

THE MODERN PHOTOGRAPH shows that the building remains largely as it was when it was first opened to the people of Wallsend over 100 years earlier, with the exception of the stunted tower, as the original spire had become unsafe and was removed. The church is now surrounded by busy roads and housing, with the modern flats visible on Park Road behind the church being built in 2004.

THE BLACK BULL HOTEL

THE BLACK BULL Hotel is pictured here in the early 1900s, looking east along High Street West, with the spire of St Luke's church visible in the distance. The Black Bull was a popular watering hole with the people of Wallsend, and bore witness to the High Street changing around it as the decades passed. The tram lines vanished as the years went by, and the buildings out of shot to the west of the hotel were demolished in the 1930s for the Ritz Cinema to be built, now a Mecca Bingo. The buildings to the east were cleared and rebuilt

as retail space in the 1960s, to coincide with the 1965 opening of The Forum shopping centre being further along High Street West (the entrance is just visible in the distance of the modern image). (Archive photograph provided by North Shields Library)

TODAY, THE BUILDING that once housed the Black Bull Hotel remains but it has passed through a number of hands, and been rebranded and reinvented in recent years. It remained the Black Bull until the late 1970s when it was renamed the Little Waster, the nickname of local stand-up comedian Bobby Thompson. It would later become the Companions Club, and then in turn was reopened as the Klub. In November 2010 it would be renamed once more as the Steam Elephant, named for a steam locomotive that was built in Wallsend. March 2013 saw the management of the beautiful old building change, and the following month it was opened as Manhattan's, complete with a new cocktail bar. The opening night saw free entertainment for those in attendance, with a Lady Gaga tribute act, the first of many as 2013 would also see Katy Perry, Adele and Robbie Williams tributes perform at the popular bar.

BRUNSWICK METHODIST CHURCH

ON EASTER MONDAY 1902 the Brunswick Methodist church on High Street East opened its doors to the people of Wallsend for the first time. The impressive building, which had cost £7,000 to build and was dubbed 'the cathedral of Wallsend' by many, had seating for 800, with an adjoining schoolroom which could comfortably accommodate 500 pupils. It had been built for the Society of Wesleyan Methodists which had previously met at a chapel on High Street West which had been built in 1883, as they'd previously had to make do with meeting at a cottage, a local public house and even a sawmill. The magnificent new building wasn't actually called the Brunswick Methodist church until 1933, as it was in this year that the Wesleyan Methodists joined the Primitive Methodists and the United Methodists to unite as the Methodist Union. The church was used until 1967 when the society was incorporated into the Station Road Methodist church, later to become known as the Trinity Methodist church. It is seen here, empty, in early 1973. (Archive photograph provided by ncjMedia Ltd)

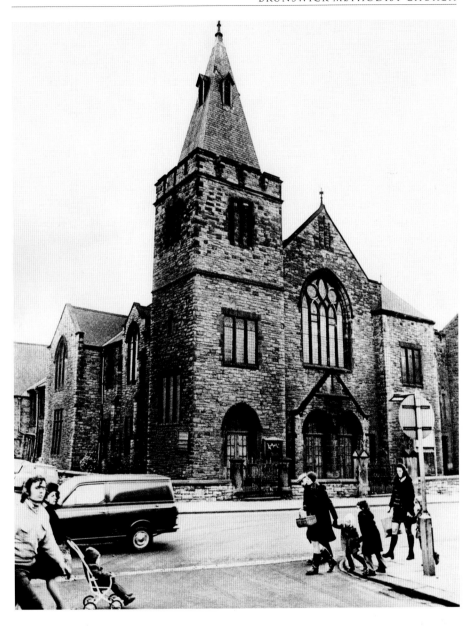

THE CHURCH, LEFT empty, lapsed into silence with no congregation to serve. Several planning applications were made; one was to use the church as a warehouse, another to convert it into a bingo hall. A London-based company put forward a proposal to use the site for shops and offices. All of these were turned down. In the winter of 1973, with no other viable proposals, the council granted planning permission to demolish Brunswick Methodist church and use the site for the erection of a three-storey block of flats with garages. Laburnum House was built in 1974 and is named due to its location on the corner of Laburnum Avenue and High Street East.

BURNS CLOSES BRIDGE

PICTURED HERE IN 1931, the Burns Closes Bridge was constructed in 1912 to link the growing communities at Rosehill and Holy Cross with Wallsend town centre. Spanning the 103m gap across Wallsend Dene, the bridge was built at a cost of £4,782 by local building firm W.T. Weir of Howdon using a new technique of creating reinforced concrete: Ferro Concrete Hennebique. The bridge was plagued with problems borne of movement of the clay strata upon which the foundations of the piers sat. In 1968 a weight limit of 12 tonnes was imposed. Over the decades, the condition of the bridge worsened and

the limit was gradually reduced until 2005 when it was closed to all road traffic. The bridge was awarded Grade II listed status in 1985; however, by 2008 the state of the bridge was beyond repair, with many locals actually fearful of crossing as the bridge was visibly unstable. In November 2008 it was demolished. A temporary pedestrian bridge was erected while building of a new £4.6 million bridge was carried out, designed by Consulting Engineers Atkins and constructed by Balfour Beatty Civil Engineering. Despite original estimates that the work would take two years, it was opened on 26 March 2009 by Geoff Hoon, Secretary of State for Transport, along with local pupil Olamide Akinropo, who had recently been elected North Tyneside Young Mayor. (Archive photograph provided by North Shields Library)

THE PRESENT-DAY bridge has two footways, one of which is wider to incorporate a cycle path, and is open to all road traffic with no restrictions.

CHURCH BANK

THIS POSTCARD IS postmarked 1913 and shows Church Bank taken from Rosehill, a popular view for postcards of the time, and it's clear to see why. In the foreground the roof of the newly opened Rose Inn is visible. A tram is heading down the bank, with a car of the period not far behind. The spire of Wallsend Secondary School and Technical Institute, which opened the following year, can be seen in the background, as can St Peter's church, for which the bank is named. Another spire can be seen beyond the

cottage, this is Church Bank Cemetery. Cottages and terraced housing further up the bank shows that Church Bank was home to many Wallsenders. Gradually, however, these homes would disappear and by the 1980s none would remain. (Archive photograph provided by North Shields Library)

THE VIEW HAS changed drastically, with woodland replacing the houses and grass on either side of the road, and it's this woodland that prevents the same view being achieved from Rosehill behind the Rose Inn, which is celebrating its centenary and is up for sale at the time of writing. Wallsend Secondary School and Technical Institute, which would later become Wallsend Grammar School and then Burnside High School, was demolished in 2004 and replaced by the £15 million Burnside Business and Enterprise College.

CHURCH OF ST MARY THE VIRGIN

THE CHURCH OF St Mary the Virgin on Churchill Street in High Howdon is part of the Willington Team of churches which also includes the Church of the Good Shepherd in Battle Hill and St Paul in Willington Quay. The church dates back to 1876, built to the design of Austin and Johnson of Newcastle. In 1987, a high-quality rood screen was installed to commemorate the Diamond Jubilee of Queen Victoria. The unique stained-glass windows show the face of Mary Burns and her daughter Mary Barbara. (Archive photograph provided by Sue McCormack)

THE TWO PHOTOGRAPHS are so different they could almost be of two different places. High Howdon has grown and developed around the church, with large houses being built on both sides of the road approaching the church, which is very much the heart of the village.

COACH AND HORSES

THE COACH AND Horses public house on High Street East dates from 1902; however, the Coach and Horses had a presence on this site from as early as 1739 when it was recorded as being a coaching inn on the turnpike road between Newcastle and North Shields. The inn was a small two-storey building with stabling for horses, and it stood almost alone in the fields between the River Tyne and Wallsend Green. The earliest recorded licensee of the Coach and Horses was in the 1840s, a coal miner named Joseph Atkinson. The original building was closed down in 1901 and the present building opened the following year; a much larger, much grander public house designed with Tudor and Jacobean stylings, combined with Classical triangle pediments and

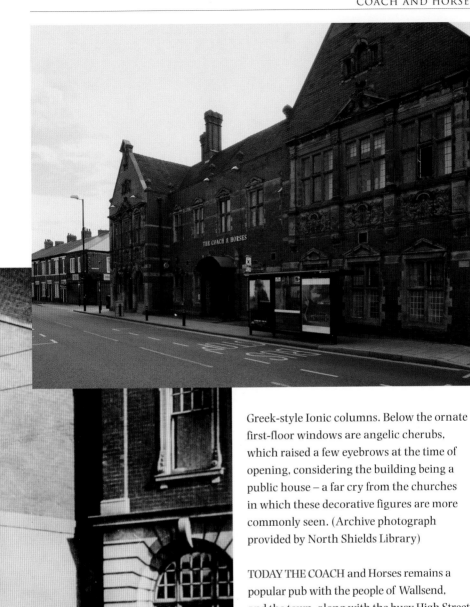

Greek-style Ionic columns. Below the ornate first-floor windows are angelic cherubs, which raised a few eyebrows at the time of opening, considering the building being a public house – a far cry from the churches in which these decorative figures are more commonly seen. (Archive photograph provided by North Shields Library)

TODAY THE COACH and Horses remains a popular pub with the people of Wallsend, and the town, along with the busy High Street East, has grown around it. The tram lines seen in the earlier 1910 photograph are long gone and have been replaced with a bus stop, conveniently placed just outside. Little has changed of the exterior of the Coach and Horses, with the exception of the lettering on the frontage of the pub replacing the original hanging sign.

CROW BANK

CROW BANK IS the small road leading downhill from the clinic on Wallsend Green to Wallsend Dene at the foot of the steep slope. Until the mid-nineteenth century the Green was made up primarily of farmhouses, and it would be a common sight to see cattle that had been grazing on the lush grass wander down the bank to drink from the burn below. This road also led to the village pump in Wallsend Dene and Holy Cross church at the north end of the Burns Closes Bridge. This image of Crow Bank dates from around 1900 and it was around this time that a 'crow shoot' was erected at the foot of the bank. It was built as a circular 6ft roofless tower in the middle of a wooded area and was designed to comfortably accommodate ten to fifteen people who would shoot at crows daring to eat seeds from their farms.

In the late 1950s the houses on Crow Bank were on the round of milkman Ernest Sumner, who would bring his 8-year-old son along at 4 a.m. every day to help deliver the milk. That 8-year-old was Gordon Sumner, who would later be better known by the name Sting and find global superstardom in the band The Police and as a solo star. (Archive photograph provided by North Shields Library)

CROW BANK HAS changed little, and the steep bank is well known to the people of Wallsend; it is this incline which leads many local sports clubs – including Wallsend RFC and running and athletics club Wallsend Harriers – to use Crow Bank as part of their training regime.

In 2008 there was outrage when workmen arrived at the crow shoot and began to pull it down. Locals frantically called North Tyneside Council in an attempt to halt the destruction of the crow shoot, the only building of its type in the North East. Eventually work was temporarily suspended but by then the tower had been reduced from its original height of 6ft down to just 3ft. The council gave the explanation that it was being demolished as the structure was unsafe. Sadly this damage was irreversible and the crow shoot has since been reduced to rubble, and lost forever.

ELM TERRACE

PICTURED HERE IN around 1910, Elm Terrace was built on Wallsend Green in 1870/71 on land created by the demolition of the farm buildings of Francis Peacock's Village Farm, which had been bought at auction in 1858 by Robert Richardson Dees of Wallsend Hall. Robert wanted his family close by and his younger brother, James William Dees, moved into No. 1 Elm Terrace and lived there until he died in 1880, but not before fathering a son, Robert Irwin Dees, in 1872.

Robert Richardson Dees took a keen interest in the people of the town and in 1897 he donated 14 acres of land for

the relaxing, socialising and exercising of the locals. Wallsend Park was opened in June 1900. When he died in 1908 he left most of his estate to his nephew, Robert Irwin Dees, who in turn passed away in 1912. The park was later renamed Richardson Dees Park in recognition of the kind donation of the land and his place in the local history of Wallsend.

In 1956, one of the houses in Elm Terrace was purchased for the purpose of being converted into a nurses' training school for the G.B. Hunter Memorial Hospital, stationed within part of Wallsend Hall. (Archive photograph provided by North Shields Library)

DESPITE THE MODERN photograph being taken around 100 years after the first, it's clear to see that Elm Terrace has changed very little in the last century. The wonderful Victorian homes are very desirable, which is hardly surprising given their location on Wallsend Green. In 2011, one of the houses in the terrace sold for over £400,000.

WALLSEND FERRY LANDING

IN FEBRUARY 1902, Hebburn-based Hawthorne, Leslie & Co. submitted a proposal to set up a ferry service to run between Wallsend and Hebburn, with the purpose of helping to get workers across the River Tyne to the shipyard in Hebburn. The Hebburn to Wallsend ferry opened in 1904, with the Wallsend ferry landing, pictured here in 1915, positioned at the end of Benton Way, and the Hebburn landing situated at the bottom of Ellison Street. Two second-hand ferries were purchased and named *Wallsend* and *Hebburn*. *Wallsend* had been built in 1890 for use on the River Clyde.

In 1939, the ferry service was no longer being used exclusively by the workers of the shipyard, so the service was taken over by Mid Tyne Ferries Ltd of Hebburn, a joint venture of Hawthorn, Leslie & Co. who started the operation, along with Wallsend shipbuilders Swan Hunter and Wigham Richardson, Walker-based shipbuilder Vickers-Armstrongs and electrical engineers A. Reyolle & Co. Two new ferries were ordered,

Mid-Tyne 1 and *Mid-Tyne 2*, and towards the end of the 1940s all four original ferries were replaced with three new diesel boats, *Tyne Queen*, *Tyne Duchess* and *Tyne Princess*. These boats were kept busy with the large number of passengers, and in summer months the ferries would run pleasure trips along the Tyne to Ryton Willows.

The Wallsend to Hebburn ferry would be immortalised forever when it appeared in the iconic 1971 film *Get Carter* starring Michael Caine. Towards the end of the 1970s, as shipbuilding on the Tyne declined, the ferry service began to operate at a loss, and in 1986 the ferry crossing closed and the boats were sold for excursion use. (Archive photograph provided by North Shields Library)

THE FERRY LANDING at Wallsend is no longer accessible, so this modern photograph was taken in Hebburn at the site of the old ferry landing at the bottom of Ellison Street, looking back across the river to Wallsend.

WALLSEND FIRE STATION

THE FIRE STATION on Lawson Street was built between 1908 and 1912 as part of the same scheme that saw the Town Hall, which the station backs onto, the baths and court either side of the fire station constructed. The municipal buildings which opened after the Town Hall are all built in a distinctive Edwardian Baroque style with red brick and sandstone.

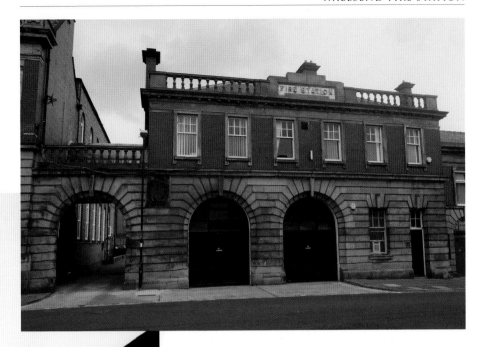

The fire station and baths are connected internally on the first-floor level. The first floor was built as a series of small rooms connected by a corridor, and the ground floor was the engine hall, with rooms for two fire engines, as can be seen here in this photograph from 1976. In the 1970s the building was extended to the rear. However, the fire station closed in the 1980s, as did the baths, with a view to build modern replacements.

Wallsend Community Fire Station opened on Hadrian Road on 27 June 1989 to replace the previous station. North Tyneside Council utilised the first floor of the now disused building as office space until 2011, when the fire station and the adjoining baths were put up for sale. The two buildings are both listed but North Tyneside Council suggest on their sales listing for the buildings that residential, office, assembly and leisure, healthcare, or any other reasonable use would be considered. (Archive photograph provided by ncjMedia Ltd)

THE BUILDING REMAINS up for sale at the time of writing, when this photograph was taken, which shows just how little the building has changed since the previous photo from 1976, and indeed since the building was opened a little over a century earlier. It now faces an uncertain future.

THE FORUM

THE YEAR 1965 saw Wallsend's first shopping centre opened to provide for the people of the rapidly expanding town. It was named The Forum shopping centre, a name chosen in recognition of the city's Roman heritage. The following year the Anson public house opened in The Forum, to replace the nearby Station Hotel. It was named after the HMS *Anson*, a 35,000-tonne battleship which launched from Swan Hunter & Wigham Richardson, later to become Swan Hunter shipyard in 1942. Another, at the time controversial, addition to The Forum was a bronze statue designed by Austrian artist and sculptor Hans Schwartz. It is called *Market Woman* and represents a hardworking Roman market trader carrying a basket full of poultry on her head. At the time of the unveiling the people of Wallsend were not impressed, and the statue was roundly criticised. These days *Market Woman* is much more appreciated, and many locals consider her to be the face of The Forum. (Archive photograph provided by ncjMedia Ltd)

THE FORUM HAS changed hugely since it opened, and is now home to forty retailers including Boots, Superdrug, Barclays Bank and Iceland. The Presto supermarket in the 1981 image has long gone and is now an indoor market. The Boots store further

along the row of shops remains; however, scaffolding now masks this row of stores. The scaffolding is part of the first stage of a major redevelopment which commenced in the summer of 2013, the biggest change in the history of the shopping centre. This will see a £5 million investment by owners NewRiver Retail to bring the rather tired building back into use for the people of Wallsend, not only as a retail experience, but also as a community destination with the addition of a state-of-the-art 50,000sq.ft library and a community centre. There will also be an additional 27,000sq.ft of retail space created and a new car park that will offer free parking for up to three hours. NewRiver Retail are also bringing The Forum into the twenty-first century when it comes to embracing technology, as free Wi-Fi will be introduced throughout the centre, and there has been the recent addition of an Amazon Locker, where people buying from the online store can have purchases delivered to a locker, making it easier to collect their items. The Forum is only the second shopping centre outside of London to include an Amazon Locker.

HIGH STREET EAST

THE MAIN SHOPPING thoroughfare in Wallsend is the High Street, which is separated into High Street West and High Street East, split by Station Road. The building in the left foreground of this photograph, taken in around 1930, is the Central Building, which was home to Boots the Chemist. The building was built in 1910 on the site of the former New Connexion church. The spire of the Brunswick Methodist church dominated the skyline and the curved building beyond is the Borough Theatre. In the foreground the building immediately on the right is Burton's the Tailors, on the corner of High Street West. (Archive photograph provided by North Shields Library)

HIGH STREET EAST in 2013 has changed a great deal. The Central Building remains, looking every bit as impressive today as it did when it was built over 100 years ago. Since Boots the Chemist ceased trading from the building there have been numerous residents and it is currently home to Ramsden's Pawnbrokers. Brunswick Methodist church is long gone, being demolished in the early 1970s and flats built upon the site. The Borough Theatre is no longer standing; in March 2011 the theatre, which had celebrated its centenary only two years earlier, was demolished and the £2.8 million Diamond House flats constructed in its place. The Heron Foods shop, seen on the right behind the traffic light, on the corner of High Street East and Station Road, is housed within a building built in 1958 and opened on 29 January the following year as Woolworths. 'Woolies' continued to trade at Nos 2-4 High Street East until the store famously closed on 2 January 2009, following the chain going into administration.

HIGH STREET WEST

HIGH STREET WEST is separated from High Street East by Station Road. High Street West is captured here around 1910. The building immediately on the left of the road is Burton's the Tailors, with the Wallsend Café situated above. The building was the vision of George Burton Hunter, the co-founder of C.S. Swan & Hunter, later to become Swan Hunter, shipyard, and who would later become Mayor of Wallsend, prior to being knighted. It was opened in 1883 and included a games room and a reading room for use of the apprentices from the shipyard. It was also the first building in Wallsend to be illuminated by electric light.

The Station Hotel can be seen on the right-hand side of the road, a popular public house with the people of Wallsend.

This crossroads was the busiest in Wallsend and policemen can be seen in the middle of the road directing the traffic of the day. (Archive Photograph provided by North Shields Library)

NOWADAYS HIGH STREET West looks very different to how it did a century ago. The building which was formerly Burton's the Tailors is now Greenways Discount Food Store. The police, who once controlled the flow of the traffic at the busy crossroads, have been replaced by traffic lights, and a speed camera can also be seen positioned just beyond the traffic light on the right.

The biggest change in the fortunes of High Street West came in the mid-1960s when the Station Hotel and the shops beyond were demolished to make way for The Forum shopping centre which opened in 1965, a move which would make High Street West the town's main shopping street and has since seen retailers such as Boots, Iceland and Superdrug open up stores within the shopping centre. The Anson public house, which can be seen in the shot, was opened the following year.

HOLY CROSS CHURCH

THE CHURCH AT Holy Cross is the earliest known church serving Wallsend. The exact date that the church was founded has been lost to time; however, historians have traced the church back to the rule of Henry II and date the church as being built in around 1155, made with stone reclaimed from the nearby Roman wall. It was built on the east side of Wallsend atop a hill overlooking the Burn Closes. It served the villages of Wallsend and Willington up until 1797. In this year the church was in the ownership of a William Clarke who was living at Wallsend Hall and decided to repair the dilapidated church. He removed the roof, as it was in dire need of being replaced. However, he abandoned the project, moving away from Wallsend and selling the church to a man named Anthony Hood. The building

was left to decay, and the missing roof only accelerated the process. It is documented that during this sorry period in the old church's history locals farmers would use the churchyard to house their horses and cows, and other villagers would remove the old gravestones from the churchyard and use them in the construction of ovens, which led to many loaves being baked with inscriptions such as 'in loving memory' and the names of those laid to rest at Holy Cross.

In 1909, following a campaign by the local people, the ruins of Holy Cross church were preserved with cement and the interior cleaned of rubble. The churchyard was reduced and the remaining gravestones moved and a metal boundary railing built around the area. During the Second World War the metal was needed to help the war effort so the railings were removed, but later restored. (Archive photograph provided by North Shields Library)

THE SITE WAS once again tidied in 1992. Today, sadly, it can be seen that the ancient monument has been scarred by graffiti.

HOWDON PARK

HOWDON PARK IS a place of recreation for the people of Howdon, in the eastern part of Wallsend. It is pictured here in the 1960s with a scene of men playing bowls on the lush green while children look on. The scene is dominated by the enormous gas holder behind them. The gasholder stands 167ft tall and was built in 1960 by Oxley Engineering to ensure there was plenty of gas to supply the people of North Tyneside even in the coldest of winters. It can store almost 3 million cu.ft of gas, enough to supply 3,600 homes for a full day, or 85,000 homes for one hour. When it was originally constructed, the gasholder, one of the largest industrial landmarks in the region, was universally hated by the people of Howdon. One newspaper described the steel structure as 'a monstrous monument in an age of ugliness'.

Howdon Park has served the people of the district over the decades with tennis courts, bowling greens and a children's play area. However, by the 1990s it had fallen into disarray and it was partly restored by the council, much to the delight of the locals. A skatepark has also been added in recent years. (Archive photograph provided by ncjMedia Ltd)

AS YOU CAN see from the present-day photograph, the controversial gas holder remains, however it appears shorter than the 1960s image and this is because the structure is built in a spiral-wound design which includes four separate sections, each with a diameter of 183ft, which lift telescopically as the holder fills with gas. In 2007 it was repainted by contractors Pyeroy in a mammoth feat which required 6,000 litres of grey paint.

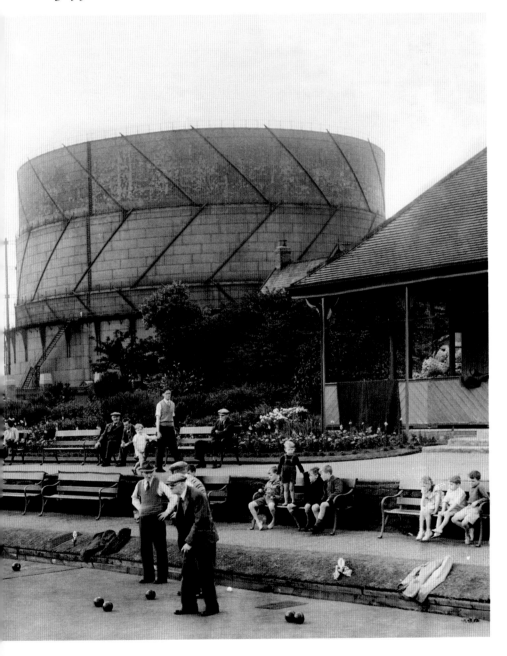

KING'S ROAD

KING'S ROAD FIRST appeared on an Ordnance Survey map in 1913, running from where the Rising Sun Sports Ground is today situated in the north, to Richardson Dees Park in the south. However, when the A1058 Coast Road was built in the 1960s, from Jesmond to Tynemouth, it split King's Road in two, creating King's Road North and King's Road South.

It's clear to see from the two photographs that this area of King's Road South has changed little over the decades, other than the style of the lampposts and the modern-day traffic-calming measures. The grand house on the left of the road is Highfield House, which in recent years was purchased for £900,000 and the enterprising buyer had it converted into five separate flats. (Archive photograph provided by North Shields Library)

IN THE BACKGROUND of the modern photograph you can see woodland – this is Richardson Dees Park, which is positioned on both sides of the road and at the time of the photograph being taken the park was undergoing a Heritage Lottery- and Big Lottery-funded 'Parks for People' restoration project.

King's Road South was in the newspapers in 2010 as locals geared up to fight to save another recreational area in the form of the former Northern Electric Sports Ground. There was a huge outcry when it closed down fourteen years prior, and the playing fields continued to be used over the years for football, cricket and rugby, and 2010 saw proposals to clear the land and build seventy-nine new houses. Despite protests and 159 letters being sent to the council, the following year saw the proposal approved by the council and building commence.

THE LYRIC CINEMA

FRIDAY, 4 AUGUST 1939 generated great excitement amongst the people of the area then known as Howdon-on-Tyne, as it was the date that the Lyric Cinema opened its doors for the first time. It was the newest cinema of the local chain Tyne Picture Houses Ltd operated by James McHarg of Wallsend. The locals came out en masse for the opening ceremony in the evening, performed by His Worship the Mayor of

Wallsend, Alderman James Paton, and the huge crowd cheered as directors, guests and the Mayor and Mayoress approached along Tynemouth Road in chauffeur-driven cars. The buzz continued inside as the invited guests and paying audience took their seats and usherettes handed out souvenir programmes. One kindly director, seeing that there were still empty seats and penniless children unable to afford the 6d fee for a seat in the stalls, ordered that the doors be opened and around fifty children be allowed in for free. The Lyric Cinema was forced to close the following month with the outbreak of the Second World War. However, it reopened within weeks, providing a welcome escape during the troubled times. (Archive photograph provided by ncjMedia Ltd)

THE LYRIC CINEMA closed its doors for the final time in early 1960 and the building today bears little resemblance to its cinema heyday. The fact it was ever a cinema at all has been largely forgotten as it now houses a Nisa Local Supermarket on the ground floor and the area which was formerly the circle is the High Howdon Social Club and Institute.

WALLSEND
MASONIC HALL

THE FOUNDATION STONE for Wallsend's Masonic Hall was laid by the Grandmaster of Northumberland, politician and statesman Sir Matthew White Ridley Bart on 1 April 1891. The hall was built for the Tyne Lodge, under the title of the Tyne Masonic Hall Co. This is the oldest known photograph of the Masonic Hall and was taken around 1906, in which year the hall was extended with the section on the left of the photograph being built, which would include the shops and dining room above. By 1935 five further lodges had joined Tyne and the Wallsend Masonic Hall Company Limited was formed. Since then many other lodges and orders have joined the company and today the Masonic Hall is a very different building in all but appearance. Originally the Masonic Hall was used only by the Freemasons and membership was by invitation only. Nowadays anyone wishing to become a Mason can sign up online and will be interviewed for suitability. (Archive photograph provided by George C. Laws)

THE MODERN PHOTOGRAPH shows that the building has changed little since the early twentieth century, although the large upstairs window has now been bricked up. The building was recently refurbished both internally and externally, but none of the original charm of this wonderful building in the heart of the city has been lost. Today the building is available to hire for functions, keep-fit classes, christenings and birthday parties.

43

NEPTUNE ROAD

NEPTUNE ROAD IS captured here in around 1910, with housing on the north side and shops further up the road including John Taylor's newsagents, Cubbon's barber shop and the Wallsend Industrial Co-operative Society. A man can be seen pushing a cart along the road. The Carville Methodist chapel is visible in the background and a crowd has gathered outside. On the south side of the road, the building in the foreground is Neptune House, which housed the Carers Centre. Tramlines can be seen on the road, beneath the overhead lines. The main tram works were stationed behind the south side of Neptune Road. (Archive photograph provided by North Shields Library)

IT'S CLEAR TO see from this modern photograph that a lot has changed in the century since the original photograph was taken. Gone are the houses on the north side of the road, as they were cleared in the 1970s and the area landscaped. Neptune House remains and still houses the Carers Centre, today named the North Tyneside Carers Centre. Another charity is based out of Neptune House: the Tyneside Community & Health Care Forum. It's a fairly busy road, with visitors to the Roman fort of Segedunum, positioned on Buddle Street just beyond the road works in the background of the shot, contributing for most of the passing traffic.

OLD POLICE STATION

WITH THE NUMBER of policemen local to
Wallsend rapidly increasing, construction
of a new police station in the centre of town
in Alexandra Street began in March 1907,
to replace the small station on High Street
West, opposite the Duke of York Inn. The new
station would house six cells and a Weights
and Measures department. There would be
an inner courtyard which would serve as
the parade ground, and the buildings that
surrounded it were houses and barracks for
the policemen, forming a square around the
perimeter when joined to the station. The people
of Wallsend were served and protected by a
total of twenty-two members of staff, made up
of a clerk, sixteen constables, three sergeants,
a detective and a superintendent. The station is

pictured here in 1915, the year in which it opened, and it served the Borough of Wallsend for almost a century before closing on 8 November 2010, following the construction of a new £23 million headquarters on Middle Engine Lane in Wallsend. This new facility covers 6 acres, has a forty-cell custody suite, and has around 275 people working there, including police officers and community support officers. (Archive photograph provided by North Shields Library)

THE MODERN-DAY photograph shows that the old police station has changed little since 1915, with the exception of the boarded-up windows and a Gateshead Council 'For Sale' sign. At the time the photograph was taken it was open to offers, with the suggestion that the building could be converted for residential purposes.

POTTER STREET

POTTER STREET, IN Willington Quay, is seen here in around 1900 and was made up of terraced housing and shops. The horse-drawn dray belongs to the Ridley, Cutter & Firth Brewery, which would be taken over by the famous Wearside-based Vaux Brewery in 1939. Deliveries are being made to the Turks Head Inn which can be seen to the left of the image, with a man in period dress walking in the door. Potter Street had another public house on the corner of the street, the Albion Inn, where local workers would often stop for breakfast. Finlay's Fish and Chips shop and Thompson's Bakery were popular with the street's residents, and other shops in Potter Street included Bainbridge Cycle Shop, a sweet shop and a hairdressers.

In the 1930s the tight-knit community of Potter Street was rocked by a decision to demolish the street in order to build Hadrian Road and develop the area for industrial use. (Archive photograph provided by North Shields Library)

POTTER STREET IS now part of the Willington Quay Industrial Estate, and is dominated by O'Brien Demolition and Dismantling and Sigma Catering Equipment. Only two buildings remain from the residential Potter Street: the Albion Inn, which was rebuilt in 1913, stands alone, split from Potter Street by Hadrian Road, and the Verne Hotel, pictured here in 2013, which is a converted section of the original terraced housing which dates back to around 1820. It had been called the Ship Hotel, before being renamed in 1986.

RICHARDSON DEES PARK

ON 4 JUNE 1900 thousands of people from all over Tyneside headed to the newly created Wallsend Park for the opening ceremony on a glorious summer's day. The co-founder of C.S. Swan & Hunter shipyard (later to become Swan Hunter), George Burton Hunter, officially opened the park to delighted onlookers. The 14 acres upon which the park had been built was donated by Robert Richardson Dees of Wallsend Hall. He had bought the former site of the C-Pit coal colliery in 1956 and donated it to the Wallsend Corporation in 1897 to be enjoyed by the people of Wallsend as somewhere they could relax, get together with friends and family and partake in exercise away from areas of the town heavily polluted by major industry.

This Valentine series postcard is dated 1909 and shows the houses on Park Road beyond the bowling greens and the original bowling pavilion, which dates from the opening of Wallsend Park nine years earlier.

In the 1960s Wallsend Park was renamed Richardson Dees Park in recognition of his original donation of the land and his important place in the local history of Wallsend.

In 2012 worked commenced on the collective Wallsend Parks, which include Richardson Dees Park, the Prince Road Arboretum and the grounds of Wallsend Hall. This multi-million pound project is part of North Tyneside Council's Excellent Parks programme and has been supported by funding from the Heritage Lottery Fund and the Big Lottery Fund's 'Parks for People' project. This work saw extensive improvements made to Richardson Dees Park, including refurbished tennis courts, creation of a new multi-use games area and restoration of historic features such as the bandstand, pavilion and the re-introduction of the Duffy Memorial Fountain. Bowling facilities were also restored and upgraded, and the pavilion was upgraded to include a café and public toilets. The lake was drained and restored, and pathways, signage and lighting were improved. (Archive photograph provided by North Shields Library)

THE VIEW HAS changed somewhat since the original 1909 postcard; the houses in Park View remain, but the pavilion has changed drastically and has also moved location so cannot be seen in this present-day photograph. The herbaceous border to the left of the original shot is now a small copse of trees behind a rockery which can be seen beyond the large noticeboard upon entering from North Road.

THE LAKE IN RICHARDSON DEES PARK

THE PICTURESQUE LAKE in Richardson Dees
Park is being enjoyed by men, women and
children in Victorian dress in the year 1900
shortly after the park, originally named Wallsend
Park, opened to be enjoyed by the people of
the town. The lake was formed at the point
of two watercourses meeting and an island
was designed in the centre of the lake for the
waterbirds to shelter.

The Victorians enjoyed creating scenic
views and it is with this in mind that the
lake was integral to the overall design of
the park. It was designed at the bottom of a

wooded valley, surrounded by steep slopes. The lake will have been a favourite haunt of many locals, who came to enjoy the tranquillity and the rich and varied wildlife. (Archive photograph provided by North Shields Library)

THIS AUTUMNAL SCENE was captured in October 2013 following the lake being inaccessible for over a year as part of a multi-million pound project is part of North Tyneside Council's Excellent Parks programme, with funding coming from the Heritage Lottery Fund and the Big Lottery Fund's 'Parks for People' project. The lake was drained, the lake and watercourses were cleaned out, and the whole area restored and improved to be enjoyed by the people of the town.

RICHARDSON DEES SCHOOL

WHEN THE SCHOOL was built in 1902 on High Street East it was named after Robert Richardson Dees. Richardson Dees was a solicitor who trained in London before returning to his native North East to set up his own practice. He bought Wallsend Hall in 1855 and took a great interest in the welfare of the town he called home. In 1897 he donated 14 acres of land for the creation of the park which would later bear his name. This postcard of the school interestingly has the name misspelt as Richardson Deis School. (Archive Photograph provided by North Shields Library)

THE SCHOOL TODAY hasn't changed much externally, although the 1980s saw it undertake some alternations and repairs. Richardson Dees Community Primary School provides a welcoming place to learn for over 250 pupils ranging in age from 3 to 11. The school was in the local news in July 2013 when children from Years 3 and 4 helped produce artwork to go on display in the entrance of the newly developed £2.8 million Diamond House flats on the site of the old Borough Theatre. The art created by the pupils linked in with the history of the site as a theatre and a cinema.

RISING SUN COLLIERY

THE RISING SUN Colliery was sunk in 1906 by the
Wallsend and Hebburn Coal Co. Ltd and coal production
began in 1908. The colliery was one of the largest
in Europe and had 60 miles of underground tunnels
stretching as far as the River Tyne. Initially coal was
transported to the surface by trucks pulled by pit ponies.
There were around eighty ponies and they were housed in
underground stables, rarely coming above the surface and
seeing the light of day. The colliery took its name from
the Rising Sun Farm, which had been situated nearby.

By 1931 there were 2,000 men working at the mine.
In 1947 coal was nationalised, and between 1953 and 1961
£2.9 million was spent on modernisation. In 1969 coal
production stopped at the colliery due to flooding problems
and the rising costs of pumping out the water, coupled with
advancements in new technology creating cheaper and

cleaner alternatives to coal. This put 1,180 men out of work and twenty-six pit ponies were made redundant.

In 1971 land reclamation started as work began on creating a country park in the heart of North Tyneside. The old colliery buildings were removed and three enormous spoil heaps that dominated the landscape were remodelled into two hills. This photograph is taken from the top of the higher of the two, the Rising Sun Hill, one of the highest points in all of Tyneside. (Archive photograph provided by Newcastle City Library)

TODAY, THE RISING Sun Country Park is a 400-acre natural retreat for the people of North Tyneside comprising of a countryside centre, an organic farm, a nature reserve, ponds and woodland. It is managed by the Rising Sun Farm Trust and North Tyneside Council. The wildlife within the park is rich with all manner of woodland creatures and visitors may be lucky enough to see foxes, badgers or even a roe deer. The park is a Site of Natural Conservation Interest (SNCI). Swallow Pond, which was formed in 1953 when mine workings collapsed, is a Local Nature Reserve (LNR). A bird hide overlooks the pond and the rare visiting birdlife makes it popular with birdwatchers.

SEGEDUNUM

SEGEDUNUM, MEANING 'STRONG fort', is the most completely excavated fort in Britain. Lying at the eastern end of Hadrian's Hall on the banks of the River Tyne, it led to the town situated within being called Wallsend. The fort covered a site of 4.1 acres and it was in use as a garrison of 600 – 120 cavalry and 480 infantry – for almost 300 years, until it was abandoned in around AD 400. The fort site was used as farmland right up until the eighteenth century when a pit village was built on the site for the miners and families of the collieries in the area. In 1884, terraced housing built for the shipyard workers completely covered the entire fort.

In the 1970s, with the terraced housing demolished, archaeologists could finally begin excavations and piece together the history of the fort which had been hidden beneath the changing landscape of Wallsend for around 1,500 years.

This photo, taken at the end of 1996, was captured during the Segedunum Project, which consisted of a series of excavations. Tyne and Wear Museum's Archaeology Projects Officer Bill Griffiths is pictured amongst the newly exposed fort. (Archive photograph provided by ncjMedia Ltd)

SEGEDUNUM ROMAN FORT, Baths & Museum was opened to the public on 17 June 2000. The public could finally see the excavated remains of the foundations of the fort, as well as a reconstructed Roman military bathhouse, giving visitors an idea of the luxury and sophistication enjoyed by the Empire almost two centuries ago on this very site.

The bathhouse is based on excavated examples at Chesters and Vindolanda forts.

The museum, with Bill Griffiths in position as curator when it opened, contains interesting finds from the archaeological digs, and the fort is brought to life with interactive exhibits and models. The centrepiece of the popular visitor attraction is a 35m-tall viewing tower which offers fantastic views, not only of the remains of the fort below but across all of Wallsend and out over the River Tyne.

ST LUKE'S CHURCH

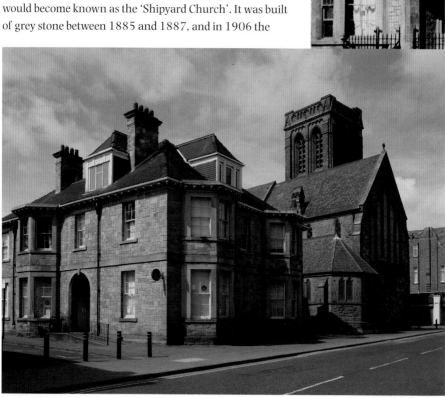

IN THE 1880s, industry, particularly shipbuilding, was growing rapidly in Wallsend and with this came the equally rapid growth of the population. The parish church of Wallsend was St Peter's and it was clear that another church was required to serve the parishioners. In 1887 the parish of St Peter's was divided; St Peter's continued to be the parish of those in the eastern end of Wallsend and those in the west would attend a new church. Land on the corner where Station Road meets Frank Street was donated by George Burton Hunter, co-founder of C.S. Swan & Hunter, later to become Swan Hunter, who also donated £1,000 towards the building of the church. Because of this generous donation the church, which would be named St Luke's church, would become known as the 'Shipyard Church'. It was built of grey stone between 1885 and 1887, and in 1906 the

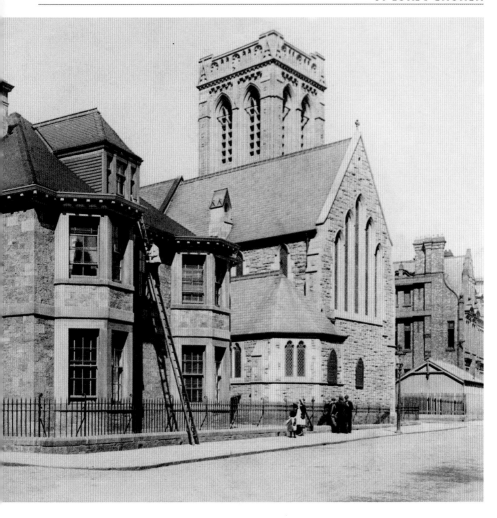

church was expanded with a 140ft-tall tower added, along with the chapel and chancel. There were plans for bells and a spire to be added, but it was discovered that the foundations were unsuitable.

The church can be seen here in a postcard postmarked 1909. The rectory can be seen in the foreground with the upstairs windows being cleaned. (Archive photograph provided by North Shields Library)

THE MODERN-DAY photograph was taken over a century after the original but, as can be seen, the church has changed little over the years, with the exception that the railings which once surrounded the church and rectory are now long gone. The east window contains a reordered Irish stained-glass window designed by Wilhelmina Geddes of Dublin and installed in 1922. It is one of the finest in Europe and is dedicated to the 269 men of the parish of St Luke's who died fighting for their country in the First World War. The rectory is now home to the Citizen's Advice Bureau.

ST PETER'S CHURCH

ST PETER'S CHURCH was consecrated on 27 April 1809, built to replace the ancient church of Holy Cross, positioned at the top of Wallsend Burn, in ruins. It may have been that the church would have been built much later, was it not for a revelation which rocked the community: in the absence of a parish church, marriages had been taking place in a schoolhouse on Wallsend Green. However, this schoolhouse was not licenced for marriages and therefore anyone who had been married there was not actually legally married, and any children born of the couple were illegitimate, which was an enormous scandal in those days. In 1807 an Act of Parliament was rushed through to legalise any marriages performed in the schoolhouse as well as approving the construction of a new church.

The new church was built on a site at the top of what is now Church Bank to a fairly simple design. In 1816 stocks were installed at the main gate to punish those who didn't attend church.

St Peter's church was Gothicised in 1892 by Newcastle architect William Searle Hicks, with the spire being removed and a new roof and windows installed. It is captured here in a postcard from 1909, the year of its centenary, when the incumbent was the Canon Charles E. Osborne. His brother was Irish poet Walter Osborne, and despite Walter's premature death in 1903, it was this connection that saw Irish artists come to St Peter's in the 1920s to create the now famous windows in the north wall. (Archive photograph provided by North Shields Library)

DESPITE THIS PHOTOGRAPH being taken over a century after the first, the church and the churchyard look remarkably similar, as very little has changed externally. Some restoration was carried out in January 1999 with funding from English Heritage and the Heritage Lottery Fund, but this work was carried out primarily on the interior of the church.

ST PETER'S RECTORY

ST PETER'S RECTORY, seen here in 1977, was built in 1852 to serve St Peter's church at the top of Church Bank and replace the old vicarage on Wallsend Green. A path from the churchyard leads to a gate in the church wall which led to the gardens of the beautiful building. In the years following the Second World War there would be a garden party held annually and before the party there would be a competition for the children of the parishioners, in which whoever could pull up the most weeds would win sixpence.

In 1980, the cost of the upkeep of the rectory was simply too much for the church, and the rectory and its gardens were sold. The Canon Peter Strange had to move temporarily to Byker until the new, smaller rectory was built and he could move back to Wallsend. (Archive photograph provided by ncjMedia Ltd)

THE ORIGINAL RECTORY was demolished by the company who bought the land. Frank Rogers, the history teacher of Burnside High School, across the road from St Peter's church, was said to have mourned the loss of the rectory.

Osborne House Retirement Home was built upon the land, offering sixty-one flats for the over 55s. The old path through St Peter's churchyard still leads to the gate in the church wall but now it offers access to the new rectory and Osborne House.

STATION ROAD

STATION ROAD IS the main route into the heart of Wallsend town centre. It is named for the train station which was opened on the street in 1939 by the Newcastle and North Shields Railway. In November 1982 it was reopened as Wallsend Metro station. The Metro station is the only public facility in Britain with Latin signage, a nod to its close proximity to the Segedunum Roman Fort.

Thomas Hedderly's Plumbers on Station Road, shown here in 1963, was opened on this site in the 1890s at which point in time Station Road was called Swan Street, due to C.S. Swan & Hunter shipyards being stationed at the end of the road on the banks of the River Tyne. Thomas Hedderly continued his father, William's, business, and it was initially a workshop to serve the two branches on High Street West in Wallsend and the

Groat Market in Newcastle. However, by the turn of the century this was their sole premises.

The development of The Forum shopping centre on the corner of High Street West and Station Road in the mid-1960s meant that not long after this photograph was taken, Thomas Hedderly's Plumbers would close for the last time. (Archive photograph provided by North Shields Library)

STATION ROAD IS a very different street to the Station Road of the 1960s. The Anson public house, which opened in 1966, is seen in the foreground. The small single-storey building with a public telephone box outside is a public toilet. Scaffolding can be seen on the large building in the background. This is part of the £5 million redevelopment of The Forum shopping centre, and this vacant, former Co-op building is being converted into a modern 50,000sq.ft library and community centre with three additional new retail units on the ground floor.

SWAN HUNTER

THE NAME SWAN Hunter is synonymous with Wallsend, and is internationally recognised as one of the world's leading shipbuilders. During a period of 130 years it has built over 1,600 ships of various types including the RMS *Mauretania*, which launched on 20 September 1906 and held the Blue Riband for the fastest crossing of the Atlantic. It also built the RMS *Carpathia*, which rescued survivors in 1912 from the most famous ship of them all, the RMS *Titanic*, as it sank in the North Atlantic after colliding with an iceberg.

The company was founded in 1880 by Wearside shipbuilder George Burton Hunter and the widow of Charles Sheridan Swan, who had been the owner of an existing shipbuilding company on Wallsend. In 1903, Swan Hunter & Wigham Richardson was born, as C.S. Swan & Hunter merged with John Wigham Richardson's shipbuilding company the Neptune Works.

This photograph captures workers leaving after their shift at the shipyard in 1977, the year in which the Swan Hunter Group was nationalised as part of British Shipbuilders.

In 1993, Swan Hunter went into receivership and it looked like the business would be broken up; however, this was averted when Jaap Kroese, a Dutch millionaire, stepped in and bought the Wallsend yard.

In 2006 the company was struggling once more, and the Royal Navy had excluded Swan Hunter from working on any of their shipbuilding projects. The land was put up for sale and the following year the iconic Swan Hunter cranes were dismantled and sold to a shipyard in India. In 2009, North Tyneside Council and One NorthEast bought up the majority of the land. Swan Hunter continued to operate from the office buildings with a workforce of just 200, focussing on design of ships, rather than the actual construction. (Archive photograph provided by ncjMedia Ltd)

AS OF 2013 Kier Property had been brought in by North Tyneside Council to regenerate the historic shipyard in a £100 million plan to convert the 34-acre site for home-advanced manufacturing companies to specialise in the offshore industry.

THE GREEN

WALLSEND GREEN DATES back as far as the ninth century. The original settlement of Wallsend had been established outside the Roman fort, but the threat of Viking raids meant that living so close to the River Tyne was no longer viable, so a new site was chosen at the present-day location of the Green. For a long time the Green consisted primarily of farms, but in the nineteenth century a number of merchants from Newcastle moved into the area, bought out the farms and built their large houses there. It became a typical English village, with a large mansion, grand houses, a schoolhouse and a vicarage, surrounding the Green in a square.

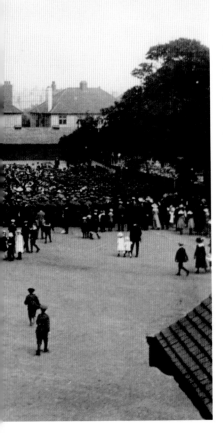

The Green was popular with the people of Wallsend, who used it as a meeting place and for social events. This photograph was taken on 4 August 1918, and the village has turned up in force on the fourth anniversary of the outbreak of the First World War. The gateway to Wallsend Hall can just be made out on the left of the photograph. The large house in the background is Dene House, built in the schoolhouse garden. The two-storey Cross House can be seen just to the left, and after that a gap can be seen before the trees. This gap is Crow Bank, leading down a steep bank to Wallsend Dene. (Archive photograph provided by North Shields Library)

WALLSEND GREEN REMAINS today as a typical village green, a far cry from the industry that the town of Wallsend is most usually associated with. It was designated a Conservation Area in 1974. The Green is much quieter these days, but it is still occasionally used for social gatherings, and the second day of 2013's Wallsend Festival was held here with folk music, medieval demonstrations, birds of prey displays and a fairground.

THE ROSE INN

THE ORIGINAL ROSE Inn, known as the old Rose Inn, pictured here in around 1900, was a coaching inn on the Newcastle to North Shields Turnpike Road. It was actually once a place of worship; in 1856, with no money available for the construction of a Catholic church, a room was rented at the old Rose Inn and mass was performed every Sunday with the congregation each paying 1s. Records show that forty-four children were baptised there by the Revd Henry Riley between 8 October 1985 and 20 May 1866, and shortly after this date a new school chapel was opened. In 1913, the old Rose Inn was demolished to make way for the new Rose Inn, which was built slightly west and further downhill than the site of the original coaching inn.

The public house has grown over the years as a community pub situated on Rosehill Bank, a busy road leading into Wallsend. (Archive photograph provided by North Shields Library)

THE ROSE INN is pictured here in 2013, the year in which it celebrates its centenary; however, as can be seen in the photograph, at this time the Rose Inn was up for sale. It remains a popular pub with the people of Wallsend and in particular the community of Rosehill. It has even found fame in recent years as being home to spirits other than those for sale behind the bar, as a ghost hunt was performed live on local radio from the historic site of the public house.

THE SHIP INN

THE SHIP INN on Gainers Terrace was more commonly known by the locals as the Ship in the Hole, to differentiate it from another pub on Wallsend's High Street West called The Ship, and because it could be reached through a pedestrian tunnel that ran below the old Riverside Railway. Located close to the Swan Hunter shipyard, it was a popular place for a quick post-work pint for the shipyard workers.

As can be seen in this photograph, the pub was on the corner of a short row of terraced houses; out of shot at the other end of the terrace was another public house named the Dock Hotel. Families who lived in the houses, and patrons at both of the two pubs, would

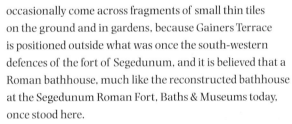

occasionally come across fragments of small thin tiles on the ground and in gardens, because Gainers Terrace is positioned outside what was once the south-western defences of the fort of Segedunum, and it is believed that a Roman bathhouse, much like the reconstructed bathhouse at the Segedunum Roman Fort, Baths & Museums today, once stood here.

The terraced houses were demolished and then in the mid-1980s the Dock Hotel was pulled down, but the Ship in the Hole continued to offer a place to drink to those who worked and lived nearby. (Archive photograph provided by Newcastle City Library)

HAVING STOOD EMPTY for a number of years, April 2013 saw the pub demolished. It was believed that it had been the oldest pub in Wallsend until this date. The site is now unused, a blank canvas waiting to be used to serve the town again. At the time of writing the future of the site is uncertain, but planning permission has been submitted by the owners of the land to build an office development.

TYNE CYCLIST AND PEDESTRIAN TUNNEL

WHEN THE TYNE Cyclist and Pedestrian Tunnel was opened by the Minister of Transport, the Right Honourable Alfred Barnes, on 24 July 1951, it became not only the first purpose-built cycling tunnel in the UK, but also the longest subterranean passages in the country. The two parallel tunnels, one for pedestrian use and a slightly wider tunnel for cyclists, run 12.2m below the bed of the River Tyne and the 270m tunnels connect Jarrow on the south side of the river with Howdon on the north. Three quarters of the £833,000 construction costs were paid by the Ministry of Transport, and the remainder by the county councils of Durham and Northumberland. The tunnels are connected at each end to single-storey rotundas. The northern rotunda is pictured here in 1967, and is

built on the site of the house where Robert Stephenson, son of railway pioneer George, was born in 1803. The buildings were connected by four escalators and a lift. The Waygood-Otis escalators have 306 wooden steps and are 60m long, with a vertical rise of 26m, making them the highest single-rise escalators in the UK at the time. The tunnels were created primarily to make commuting to work easier for the thousands of shipyard and industrial workers who lived on the north and south banks at the time. The tunnel was free and was used by 20,000 people a day. When the road Tyne Tunnel opened in 1967, usage of the Tyne Cyclist and Pedestrian Tunnel reduced, and as the shipbuilding industry declined over the decades as did the number of people passing through the tunnel on a daily basis. Today, around 20,000 use the tunnels each month. In 2000 the tunnels were awarded a Grade II listed status. (Archive photograph provided by Newcastle City Library)

THIS TUNNEL IS currently being refurbished in a £4.9 million project which will include new lighting, installation of CCTV, repairs to the tiling and panelling and modern signage. Externally the rotundas will have renovation carried out to the original windows, and the roofs will be repaired and repainted, restoring them back to the original light grey colour. The most radical change will see two of the famous wooden escalators, which regularly break down and are beyond economical repair, replaced with inclined glass lifts. The two remaining wooden escalators will be preserved *in situ*, with feature lighting to give tunnel users a chance to marvel at their construction and operation.

VILLAGE PUMP

IT IS UNCERTAIN exactly when Wallsend's village pump was constructed, but it is believed to have been in the early 1800s. Positioned in Wallsend Dene, in the heart of the town, and close to the farmsteads on Wallsend Green, the pump was the source of water for all of the town's needs. The pump was considered so central to village life that, in 1914, when a local team that played in a Tyneside amateur league were having a team photograph taken they posed around the village pump. This photograph was taken in 1915 and shows the

pump complete and in working order.
(Archive photograph provided by
North Shields Library)

AS THE DECADES passed by,
and internal plumbing in people's
homes became the norm, the village
pump became redundant, and decay
and vandalism has led to only the
base remaining and can be seen
in this present-day photograph.
Sadly, even the base has not escaped
vandalism and has suffered from
graffiti. It's largely ignored by the
dog walkers and passers-by these
days, with few realising the vital
part the village pump played in
the history of Wallsend, often
mistaking it for nothing more
than an old section of wall.

WALLSEND
BOWLING GREEN

THIS SCENE SHOWS Wallsend bowling green in Richardson Dees Park in a postcard postmarked 1917. Despite the constant worry of the First World War, men from Wallsend are enjoying a game of bowls in period dress, and children can be seen in the foreground looking on. In the background the houses on North Road can be seen, as can the spire of the Allen Memorial Methodist church on the corner of North Road and Park Road.

There has been an active bowling community within Wallsend, enjoying the bowling green, for over 100 years, and the Wallsend Borough Bowling Club was founded on 27 September 1922. The club would become very successful playing their matches on the bowling green in the park. In 2010, the two Wallsend bowls clubs, the Wallsend Borough Bowling Club and the Wallsend Bowling Club, merged to form the Wallsend Park Bowling Club.

Richardson Dees Park has recently undergone a multi-million pound transformation, funded by North Tyneside Council in conjunction with the Heritage Lottery Fund and the Big Lottery Fund 'Parks for People' project. This included improvements to the bowling facilities, including the introduction of a café and public toilets into the pavilion and the greens restored, and, as can be seen in this photo, next to the mechanical digger is the partially completed re-installation of the Duffy Memorial Fountain between the greens. The fountain was originally unveiled in 1912 in memory of community leader Joseph Duffy. Duffy opened a brick works in the town in 1884, and his legacy grew as he built much of the old Buddle Ward and owned the Wallsend Borough Theatre on High Street East. In 1901, Wallsend officially became a borough and Duffy was elected onto the council and became Mayor in 1909, but sadly passed away the following year. The fountain was designed in his memory by local architects Benjamin F. Simpson and Sidney H. Lawson, and given pride of place in Richardson Dees Park. However, it was later removed and was found in pieces in Burns Close. (Archive photograph provided by North Shields Library)

THIS REBUILT FOUNTAIN is being constructed based on photographs and measurements of the original. The houses on North Road remain, as does the Allen Memorial Methodist church, although its spire has been removed as it became unsafe. They are mostly obscured by the trees which line the perimeter of the park.

WALLSEND
BOYS' CLUB

WALLSEND BOYS' CLUB was founded on 14 November 1904 by the employees and directors of Swan Hunter & Wigham Richardson shipyards (later to become Swan Hunter) to give their apprentices somewhere to spend recreational time. Club activities in the early years included boxing, snooker, trampolining, judo, cross-country running, drama and football.

During the 1930s new members joined the club from engineering, mining and other heavy industries in the area. The first club building was constructed in 1938 as a series of wooden huts on nearby Station Road, erected by workers from the shipyard. It was opened in 1939 and lasted twenty years until it was gutted beyond repair by fire on 9 June 1959.

In 1964 work commenced on a replacement club building, pictured here in 1966; the year in which it was opened. An opening ceremony took place on Friday 16 December, where the Duke of Northumberland conducted the official opening of what was described as 'the best club building in the north of England'. (Archive photograph provided by Michael McGill)

ALTHOUGH THE CLUB has run a varied array of activities for the members, it has found fame for producing professional footballers, with over sixty-five players from the club going on to play professionally. Players who once wore the colours of Wallsend Boys' Club and made the grade in the professional game include Peter Beardsley, Steve Bruce, Michael Carrick, Steve Watson, Steven Taylor and Newcastle United and Premier League record goal-scorer Alan Shearer.

Wallsend Boys' Club was awarded the Freedom of the City of North Tyneside in 2008 in recognition of the club's community work and what the Deputy Mayor described as its 'factory line of talent'.

In 2011, the club opened a football centre on Rheydt Avenue; the £1.4 million site would give the club it's very own pitches, whereas previously they'd played on local park pitches. The facility consists of two full-size pitches, five junior pitches, one mini-soccer-size pitch and a changing pavilion (pictured here).

The Station Road building continued to act as the headquarters for the club until January 2012, when it was damaged by high winds, destroying one of the walls. It was demolished in February and March and the site is now being used to build twelve council houses, the first council houses to be constructed in Wallsend since 1989.

WALLSEND DENE

IT IS ALMOST impossible to tell where exactly in Wallsend Dene these locals are enjoying a sit down in the woodland in days long past, but it's safe to say that this ancient grassland has been enjoyed by the people of Wallsend for centuries – whether it be bringing cattle to graze or fetching water from the village pump, the Dene has remained a constant as the town of Wallsend has developed and expanded in every direction around it.

The Dene is a rich conservation resource and one of the most important and diverse in all of North Tyneside, with the grassland and scrub home to a myriad of flora and fauna, and the Wallsend Burn linking the River Tyne to the heart of Wallsend.

Burns Close Pasture is found beneath and to either side of Burns Closes Bridge and it is one of the few remaining semi-natural areas of grassland in North Tyneside. It has huge

conservational value and contains many plant species
uncommon to the area and most often found in areas
of unimproved grassland; common fleabane, smooth
tare, pepper saxifrage, bee orchid and dyer's greenwood.
This plant life helps to support the significant population of
butterflies including the common blue and meadow brown.
The birdlife to be found in the Dene include the dunnock,
linnet and great tit, utilising the scrub as breeding sites. It's
not uncommon to see the awesome sight of a sparrowhawk
hovering overhead in the hope of spotting prey in the shape
of the small mammals that can be found here, such as
the field vole. (Archive photograph provided by Newcastle
City Library)

IN 2005, WALLSEND Dene was designated a Local Nature
Reserve (LNR) site and immediately it was identified that
work was required to make Wallsend Burn more wildlife
friendly. This was completed in March 2010.

Wallsend Dene is a hugely popular place for people to
enjoy walking and cycling, as can be seen here in this
modern photograph. The base of the old village pump can be
seen in the background.

WALLSEND HALL

WALLSEND HALL HAS been the largest and grandest home in all of Wallsend ever since it was built to face the picturesque Wallsend Green in the early 1800s, although it's believed that it was built on the site of a previous mansion dating back to the 1600s.

Many prominent figures from Wallsend's history have called Wallsend Hall home, including Robert Richardson Dees, for whom the local park is named, and Sir George Burton Hunter, co-founder of the Swan Hunter shipyard.

It was Sir George Burton Hunter who donated the hall and its grounds to the council in 1916 providing they were used for the people of Wallsend. Later, a further agreement was made that part of the building could be used as a hospital, which would include a maternity department and would be named the G.B. Hunter Memorial Hospital.

This photograph was taken in the 1950s, at which time the building was still being used partially as a hospital and the remainder for civic functions. (Archive photograph provided by North Shields Library)

WITH THE EXCEPTION of the large green in the centre of the grass and the car park in front of the building, the two images differ very little. However, the building is now privately owned and is used as a tea room, and is available for hire as the perfect venue for weddings and conferences.

The hall's grounds have recently been part of the mult-million pound regeneration of Wallsend Parks, and they are still enjoyed by the people of Wallsend. The 9 acres of mature woodland with riverside walks are popular with dog walkers and people simply enjoying the tranquil grounds and beautiful surroundings.

WALLSEND SECONDARY SCHOOL AND TECHNICAL INSTITUTE

WALLSEND SECONDARY SCHOOL and Technical Institute opened on 23 September 1914 and the first head teachers were a Miss E. Giles and Walter Bretney. In 1944 it was renamed Wallsend Grammar School.

On 15 July 1960 a separate building was opened by the Chairman of Parsons in the grounds of the existing grammar school; this was called the Wallsend County Technical School and was designed for 660 students from age 11, as well as accommodating a sixth form programme. The building of this technical school came from a need to accommodate the additional volume of students born of the post-war baby boom.

On 3 September 1969 the two separate schools were united as Burnside High School, a comprehensive high school with an initial roll of 970 students between the age of 13-18 and fifty-six members of staff.

Notable alumni of the school are professional rugby players Chris Thorman and Micky Ward, footballers Steve Watson and Michael Carrick, and *Geordie Shore*'s Vicky Pattison. (Archive photograph provided by North Shields Library)

THE ORIGINAL BUILDINGS were demolished in 2004 and the new £15 million Burnside Business and Enterprise College, which had been built behind the original school, was opened in September, later being inaugurated by Queen Elizabeth II. The new college was constructed by Kajima, a Japanese construction company, and was designed to combine modern architecture with Wallsend's Roman heritage with a basis on a Roman Mile Castle, which would have been stationed at every mile along Hadrian's Wall.

In 2009 work began on the Hadrian Leisure Centre in the grounds of the college. Costing £7 million it was opened the following year and offers students and local people the chance to utilise the facilities, which include a 25m pool, a smaller learning pool, a fitness suite, a climbing wall, a multi-use sports hall and a variety of outdoor facilities.

WALLSEND TOWN HALL

WALLSEND WAS GRANTED borough status in 1901, and shortly afterwards the
Wallsend Borough Council was formed. The previous year land on the High Street had
been acquired for the building of a town hall. The council of 'new' Wallsend met in
the Masonic Hall on Hugh Street in those early years, and on 19 February 1907 the
foundation stone was laid of the impressive Town Hall designed by Liddle & Brown of
Newcastle, and constructed by W. Franklin & Sons.

On 16 September 1908, Wallsend Town Hall and the Municipal Buildings, which included the fire station on Lawson Street and the public baths, were officially opened. The illuminated clock was presented to the council by the newly appointed first Mayor of the Borough of Wallsend, William Boyd, back in 1901 but not started until the opening ceremony. (Archive photograph provided by North Shields Library)

WALLSEND TOWN HALL is now the headquarters of North Tyneside Council and, as can be seen when comparing the earlier postcard postmarked 1916 with the modern-day photograph, the building has changed very little externally over the years, with the exception of the removal of the railings which once surrounded the building. The clock on the front of the building is still in working order. In 2005 it was removed as there were concerns about the cast-iron surround corroding and potentially falling from the building. Experts restored the clock with costs of around £10,000, before replacing the clock back in its original position, although it no longer illuminates after dark.

WILLINGTON MILL

WILLINGTON MILL IS one of the oldest remaining industrial buildings in Wallsend. A small flour mill was original built on the site on a bend in Willington Gut in the mid-1700s by William Brown. He went into business with two Quakers named Joseph Proctor and Joseph Unthank, and they replaced the small mill with the current building as one of Britain's first steam-powered flour mills.

It became infamous in the early nineteenth century as one of the most haunted buildings in the north of the country. Joseph Proctor Jnr moved into the house that can be seen to the left of the seven-storey mill in this photograph, taken around 1899, and kept a diary of terrifying

happenings that beset himself and his family until they had enough and moved out in 1947, having called the haunted mill complex home for sixteen years. Locals began to call the mill Kitty's Mill, as it was believed that this was the name of the ghost that roamed Willington Mill. (Archive photograph provided by North Shields Library)

TODAY, WILLINGTON MILL still bears the nickname of Kitty's Mill, and as can be seen in this photograph the only building that remains from the original nineteenth-century image is the seven-storey mill, although it has since been reduced to four storeys and has a curved roof. It is now a listed building and acts as the canteen for the newer rope work buildings.

WILLINGTON VIADUCT

THE WILLINGTON VIADUCT was built between 1837 and 1839 to designs by John and Benjamin Green, celebrated father and son architects of Newcastle-upon-Tyne, who designed many landmarks in the area such as Grey's Monument and the Theatre Royal in Newcastle city centre, and Penshaw Monument in Durham. It was built using the Wiebeking system of using laminated timber, one of the earliest bridges in Britain constructed this way. The 1,048ft long, 82ft high bridge was built to serve the Newcastle and North Shield's Railway Company, as was its sister bridge, the Ouseburn Viaduct at Byker.

In 1845, the Newcastle and North Shields Railway Company was amalgamated into the Newcastle and

Berwick Railway, and, in 1869, the bridge was rebuilt to the original designs in iron by the Weardale Iron and Coal Company, as was the bridge at the Ouseburn. (Archive photograph provided by Newcastle City Library)

THE VIADUCT HAS changed little, and the train that can be seen crossing it is a Tyne and Wear Metro. The 'Metro' as it's known locally opened in 1980 and has expanded to serve Newcastle, Gateshead, North Tyneside, South Tyneside and Sunderland.

If you enjoyed this book, you may also be interested in …

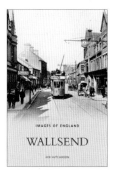

Wallsend

KEN HUTCHINSON

A wonderfully nostalgic glimpse at the Wallsend of yesteryear through a collection of 200 archive photographs accompanied by informative and memory-provoking captions.

978 0 7524 3424 7

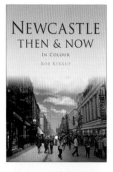

Newcastle Then & Now

ROB KIRKUP

The city of Newcastle has a rich heritage, which is uniquely reflected in this delightful, full-colour compilation. Contrasting a selection of forty-five archive images alongside modern photographs taken from the same location, this book reveals the changing faces, buildings and streets of Newcastle during the last century. *Newcastle Then & Now* provides a glimpse of how the city used to be, awakening nostalgic memories for those who live or work here.

978 0 7524 6566 1

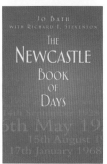

The Newcastle Book of Days

JO BATH & RICHARD F. STEVENSON

Taking you through the year day by day, *The Newcastle Book of Days* contains quirky, eccentric, amusing and important events and facts from different periods in the history of the city. Featuring hundreds of snippets of information gleaned from the vaults of Newcastle's archives and covering the social, criminal, political, religious, industrial, military and sporting history of the region, this book will delight residents and visitors alike.

978 0 7524 6866 2

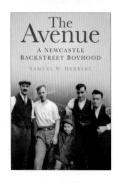

The Avenue: A Newcastle Backstreet Boyhood

SAMUEL W. HERBERT

This is a hard-hitting account of growing up in Newcastle's West End during the uncertain years of the First World War and the Depression. Samuel Herbert had to grow up fast when his mother moved the family to a cockroach-infested tenement in Elswick while his Dad was away fighting on the front line. Along with the tragedy, however, came lots of laughs, and Samuel's unique account demonstrates the humour, courage and indomitable spirit of the local population. These stories vividly capture the heart and heritage of this former mining community.

978 0 7524 6886 0

Visit our website and discover thousands of other History Press books.

www.thehistorypress.co.uk